BOOKS BY PHILIP LEVINE

A WALK WITH TOM JEFFERSON 1988

SWEET WILL 1985

SELECTED POEMS 1984

ONE FOR THE ROSE 1981

7 YEARS FROM SOMEWHERE 1979

ASHES: POEMS NEW AND OLD 1979

THE NAMES OF THE LOST 1976

1933 1974

THEY FEED THEY LION 1972

RED DUST 1971

PILI'S WALL 1971

NOT THIS PIG 1968

ON THE EDGE 1963

A WALK WITH
TOM JEFFERSON

A WALK WITH TOM JEFFERSON

POEMS BY

PHILIP LEVINE

ALFRED A. KNOPF NEW YORK 1988

Some poems in this work were originally published in the following publications: *Michigan Quarterly Review*, *The Missouri Review*, *The New Yorker*, *Ohio Review*, *The Paris Review*, *The Partisan Review*, and *Western Humanities Review*. "I Sing the Body Electric" was originally published in *Antaeus*. "Dog Poem" was originally published in *The Gettysburg Review*. "These Streets" was originally published in *The Hudson Review*. "Picture Postcard from the Other World" was originally published in *Ploughshares*. "Winter Words," "The Whole Soul" and "For the Country" were originally published in *Poetry*.

Library of Congress Cataloging-in-Publication Data

Levine, Philip, [date]
    A walk with Tom Jefferson.

I. Title.
PS3562.E9W35   1988   811'.54   87–46080
ISBN 0-394-57038-3
ISBN 0-394-75859-5 (pbk.)

FOR T.J. ANDERSON
WHO GETS THE MUSIC

CONTENTS

I

Buying and Selling   3
Making Light of It   5
Winter Words   6
The Rat of Faith   10
The Whole Soul   12
28   14

II

Bitterness   21
Making it Work   22
Another Song   23
Waking in March   24
For the Country   25
These Streets   31

III

At Bessemer   37
Dog Poem   38
Theory of Prosody   40
In a Light Time   41
I Sing the Body Electric   43
Picture Postcard from the Other World   45

IV

A Walk with Tom Jefferson   49

I

BUYING AND SELLING

All the way across the Bay Bridge I sang
to the cool winds buffeting my Ford,
for I was on my way to a life of buying
untouched drive shafts, universal joints,
perfect bearings so steeped in Cosmoline
they could endure a century and still retain
their purity of functional design, they
could outlast everything until like us
their usefulness became legend and they
were transformed into sculpture. At Benicia
or the Oakland Naval Yard or Alameda
I left the brilliant Western sun behind
to enter the wilderness of warehouses
with one sullen enlisted man as guide.
There under the blinking artificial light
I was allowed to unwrap a single sample,
to hack or saw my way with delicacy
through layer after layer of cardboard,
metallic paper, cloth webbing, wax
as hard as wood until the dulled steel
was revealed beneath. I read, if I could,
the maker's name, letters, numbers,
all of which translated into functions
and values known only to the old moguls
of the great international junk companies
of Chicago, Philadelphia, Brooklyn,
whose young emissary I was. I, who at
twenty had wept publicly in the Dexter-
Davison branch of the public library
over the death of Keats in the Colvin
biography and had prayed like him
to be among the immortals, now lived
at thirty by a code of figures so arcane
they passed from one side of the brain
to the other only in darkness. I, who
at twenty-six had abandoned several careers
in salesmanship— copper kitchenware,

Fuller brushes, American encyclopedias—
from door to unanswered door in the down
and out neighborhoods of Detroit, turning
in my sample cases like a general handing
over his side arms and swagger stick, I
now relayed the new gospels across mountains
and the Great Plains states to my waiting masters.
The news came back: Bid! And we did
and did so in secret. The bids were
awarded, so trucks were dispatched,
Mohawks, Tam O'Shanters, Iroquois.
In new Wellingtons, I stood to one side
while the fork lifts did their work,
entering only at the final moment to pay
both loaders and drivers their pittances
not to steal, to buy at last what could
not be bought. The day was closing down.
Even in California the afternoon skies
must turn from blue to a darker blue
and finally take the color of coal, and stars
—the same or similar ones—hidden so long
above the Chicago River or the IRT
to Brooklyn, emerge stubbornly not in ones
but in pairs, for there is safety in numbers.
Silent, alone, I would stand in the truck's
gray wake feeling something had passed,
was over, complete. The great metal doors
of the loading dock crashed down, and in
the sudden aftermath I inhaled a sadness
stronger than my Lucky Strike, stronger
than the sadness of these hills and valleys
with their secret ponds and streams unknown
even to children, or the sadness of children
themselves, who having been abandoned believe
their parents will return before dark.

MAKING LIGHT OF IT

I call out a secret name, the name
of the angel who guards my sleep,
and light grows in the east, a new light
like no other, as soft as the petals
of the blown rose of late summer.
Yes, it is late summer in the West.
Even the grasses climbing the Sierras
reach for the next outcropping of rock
with tough, burned fingers. The thistle
sheds its royal robes and quivers
awake in the hot winds off the sun.
A cloudless sky fills my room, the room
I was born in and where my father sleeps
his long dark sleep guarding the name
he shared with me. I can follow the day
to the black rags and corners it will
scatter to because someone always
goes ahead burning the little candle
of his breath, making light of it all.

WINTER WORDS

For Tu Fu

Day after day in a high room between
two rivers, I sit alone and welcome
morning across the junked roof tops
of Harlem. Fifteen stories up, neither
on a cloud of soot nor a roof of stone,
I am in my element, urging the past
out of its pockets of silence.
                              The friends
of my first poems long banished
into silence and no time, leaving nothing
to tell me who they are.
                              A nail of sunlight
on the George Washington Bridge. The first cars
crossing to the island douse their lights
and keep coming. They'll be joining us,
these early risers from New Jersey.

*

Sheets of rain falling in the descending
evening dark. Red lights of the chicken shack
at Manhattan and 125th. The bridge lights,
green and white. A siren comes on yelping,
and another. The rain doubles and smears
the night across the wide world.
                              Years ago
by the mudflats of the Llobregat
we walked in the late mist. Wild bird cry
from a shivering stand of bamboo.
The high voices of young women and girls
as they gathered the long day's remnants.
In the half-dark a child found three feathers
of a kingfisher and took them as a gift
of nature and gave me one.
                              I hold it
now on my open palm for a moment.

It rises slowly and settles on no wind
but my breathing, the colors softened
to the usual shades of rain, night, sleep.

*

From where I stand the Hudson barely moves—
over an hour and nothing has passed
up or down. I can see a few tugs smoking
on the Jersey side, and when the sky lifts
gray daylight falls on barges, warehouses,
rail yards, black mountains of tenements,
the smoking stacks of factories.
                                        Once I slept
beside a wide river whose currents pulled
both night and day. I thought it began
at the source of all sweet waters and took them
through seven small seas to a great ocean
tasting of salt and our lives.
                              When the sun breaks
through the full clouds of boyhood, we are there
waiting on the dock in our summer suits
for bright lake boats with the names of islands.

*

Birthday tulips, twelve hothouse flowers
of royal purple on long stilt-like legs
that sag beside the frosted window.
Paper white narcissus uncoiled from bulbs
that had only polished stones to push
their green shoots through. You can grow up here.

East I can see to Throg's Neck, a pale bridge
that leads to Connecticut, and above
the bridge a skyway of air the birds
could take if they wanted another world.

Down below in an empty parking lot
I find my favorite, the sparrow
who picks about the gravel, and he invites
me in with a twist of his head, a knock
of his beak. You can grow down here.

*

Snow flakes racing across my window,
then wind-checked, reversed, wheeling
back east to west.
                          At Puigcerda
on the way back from the holy valley
of Andorra, clouds of black starlings
rising at dusk from bare winter trees
and the hard ashen fields of December,
a twisting cloud above the road. They knew
where they were going.
                                    Still more snow until
slowly the dark rooftops below erase
their sullen faces. One lost seagull
against a featureless gray sky,
white wings extended, hung
motionless above the changing winds.

*

Above the bridge lights a rope of stars.
Alone, late at night, my breath fogging
the window, I can almost believe
the sleeping world is the reflection
of heaven.
                    Detroit, 1951,
Friday night, after swing shift we drove
the narrow, unmarked country roads searching
for Lake Erie's Canadian shore.
Later, wrapped in rough blankets, barefoot

on a private shoal of ground stones
we watched the stars vanish as the light
of the world rose slowly from the great
gray inland sea. Wet, shivering, raised
our beer cans to the long seasons
to come. We would never die.
       Scattered
to distant shores, long ago gone back
to the oily earth of Ohio,
the carved Kentucky hills, the smokeless air.

THE RAT OF FAITH

A blue jay poses on a stake
meant to support an apple tree
newly planted. A strong wind
on this clear cold morning
barely ruffles his tail feathers.
When he turns his attention
toward me, I face his eyes
without blinking. A week ago
my wife called me to come see
this same bird chase a rat
into the thick leaves
of an orange tree. We came as
close as we could and watched
the rat dig his way into an orange,
claws working meticulously.
Then he feasted, face deep
into the meal, and afterwards
washed himself in juice, paws
scrubbing soberly. Surprised
by the whiteness of the belly,
how open it was and vulnerable,
I suggested I fetch my .22.
She said, "Do you want to kill him?"
I didn't. There are oranges
enough for him, the jays, and us,
across the fence in the yard
next door oranges rotting
on the ground. There is power
in the name *rat*, a horror
that may be private. When I
was a boy and heir to tales
of savagery, of sleeping men
and kids eaten half away before
they could wake, I came to know
that horror. I was afraid
that left alive the animal
would invade my sleep, grown

immense now and powerful
with the need to eat flesh.
I was wrong. Night after night
I wake from dreams of a city
like no other, the bright city
of beauty I thought I'd lost
when I lost my faith that one day
we would come into our lives.
The wind gusts and calms
shaking this miniature budding
apple tree that in three months
has taken to the hard clay
of our front yard. In one hop
the jay turns his back on me,
dips as though about to drink
the air itself, and flies.

THE WHOLE SOUL

Is it long as a noodle
or fat as an egg? Is it
lumpy like a potato or
ringed like an oak or an
onion and like the onion
the same as you go toward
the core? That would be
suitable, for is it not
the human core and the rest
meant either to keep it
warm or cold depending
on the season or just who
you're talking to, the rest
a means of getting it from
one place to another, for it
must go on two legs down
the stairs and out the front
door, it must greet the sun
with a sigh of pleasure as
it stands on the front porch
considering the day's agenda.
Whether to go straight ahead
passing through the ranch houses
of the rich, living rooms
panelled with a veneer of fake
Philippine mahogany and bedrooms
with ermined floors and tangled
seas of silk sheets, through
adobe walls and secret gardens
of sweet corn and marijuana
until it crosses several sets
of tracks, four freeways, and
a mountain range and faces
a great ocean each drop of
which is known and like
no other, each with its own
particular tang, one suitable

to bring forth the flavor
of a noodle, still another
when dried on an open palm,
sparkling and tiny, just right
for a bite of ripe tomato
or to incite a heavy tongue
that dragged across a brow
could utter the awful words,
"Oh, my love!" and mean them.
The more one considers
the more puzzling become
these shapes. I stare out
at the Pacific and wonder—
noodle, onion, lump, double
yoked egg on two legs,
a star as perfect as salt—
and my own shape a compound
of so many lengths, lumps,
and flat palms. And while I'm
here at the shore I bow to
take a few handfuls of water
which run between my fingers,
those poor noodles good for
holding nothing for long, and
I speak in a tongue hungering
for salt and water without salt,
I give a shape to the air going
out and the air coming in,
and the sea winds scatter it
like so many burning crystals
settling on the evening ocean.

At 28 I was still faithless.
I had crossed the country in a green Ford,
sleeping one night almost 14 hours in a motel
above Salt Lake City. I discovered
I'd had a fever all that day and thus the animals
that dotted the road, the small black spots
that formed and unformed crows, the flying pieces
of slate that threatened to break through
the windshield . . . were whatever they were.
I took two aspirins and an allergy pill—that was all
I had—and got into bed although it was light out.
That was 28 years ago. Since then I have died
only twice, once in slow motion against
the steel blue driver's side of a Plymouth
station wagon. One moment before impact I said
to myself, seriously, "This is going to hurt."
The kids in the Plymouth's back seat gaped
wildly, shouted, leaped, and the father held firm
to the steering wheel as I slipped through the space
that was theirs, untouched, skidding first
on the black field of asphalt and broken glass
that is California 168, Tollhouse Road, and over
the edge of the mountain, the motorcycle
tumbling off on its own through nettles and grass
to come to a broken rest as all bodies must.
Often when I shave before a late dinner, especially
on summer evenings, I notice the white lines
on my right shoulder like the smeared imprint
of a leaf on silk or the delicate tracings
on a whale's fins that the smaller sea animals carve
to test his virtue, and I reenter the wide blue eyes
of that family of five that passed on their way
up the mountain.
                        But at 28 I was still faithless.
I could rise before dawn from a bed drenched
with my own sweat, repack the green Ford
in the dark, my own breath steaming

in the high, clear air, and head for California.
I could spend the next night in Squaw Valley
writing a letter to my wife and kids asleep hours
behind me in Colorado, I could listen to Rexroth
reminiscing on a Berkeley FM station in the voice
God uses to lecture Jesus Christ and still believe
two aspirins, an allergy pill, and proper rest were proof
against the cold that leaps in one blind moment
from the heart to the farthest shore to shudder
through the small sea creatures I never knew existed.

It seems the sun passing back and forth behind clouds
this morning threatens to withdraw its affections
and the sky is as distant and pale as a bored child
in the wrong classroom or a man of 28
drilled so often on the names of fruit-bearing trees
that he forgets even the date palm. Here in New England,
no longer new or English, the first frost
has stained the elms and maples outside my window,
and the kids on their way hunch their shoulders
against the cold. One boy drops his lunch box
with a clatter and mysteriously leaves it there
on the pavement as a subtle rebuke
to his mother, to a father holding tight to a wheel,
to a blue Plymouth that long ago entered the heaven
brooding above Detroit. If only they had stopped
all those years ago and become a family of five
descending one after the other the stone ledges
of Sweet Potato Mountain and found me face down
among the thistles and shale and lifted me to my feet.
I weighed no more than feathers do or the wish
to become pure spirit. If I had not broken my glasses
I could have gone on my way with a thank you,
with a gap-toothed smile.
                    28 years ago, faithless, I
found the great bay of San Francisco where the map
said it would be and crossed the bridge from Oakland

singing "I Cover the Waterfront" into the cold winds
and the dense odor of coffee. Before I settled
in East Palo Alto among divorcees and appliance salesmen,
fifty yards from the Union Pacific tracks, I spent a long weekend
with Arthur, my mentor to be. In a voice ruined, he said,
by all-night draughts of whiskey and coffee, he praised
the nobility of his lemon and orange trees, the tang
of his loquats, the archaic power of his figs.
In a gambler's green visor and stiff Levis, he bowed
to his wounded tomatoes swelling into late summer.
Kneeling in the parched loam by the high fence
he bared the elusive strawberries, his blunt fingers
working the stiff leaves over and over. It was August.
He was almost happy.
                           Faithless, I had not found
the olive trees bursting on the hillsides west
of US 99. I knew only the bitter black fruit
that clings with all its life to the hard seed.
I had not wakened to mockers wrangling in my yard
at dawn in a riot of sexual splendor or heard
the sea roar at Bondy Bay, the long fingers
of ocean running underneath the house all night
to rinse off the pain of nightmare. I had not
seen my final child, though he was on the way.
I had not become a family of five nor opened
my arms to receive the black gifts of a mountain road,
of ground cinders, pebbles, rough grass.
                                    At twice my age
Arthur, too, was faithless, or so he insisted
through the long sober evenings in Los Altos, once
crowded with the cries of coyotes. His face
darkened and his fists shook when he spoke
of Nothing, what he would become in that waiting blaze
of final cold, a whiteness like no other.
At 56, more scared of me than I of him,
his right forefinger raised to keep the beat,
he gravelled out his two great gifts of truth:

"I'd rather die than reread the last novels
of Henry James," and, "Philip, we must never lie
or we shall lose our souls." All one winter afternoon
he chanted in Breton French the coarse poems of Tristan Corbière,
his voice reaching into unforeseen sweetness, both hands
rising toward the ceiling, the tears held back so long
still held back, for he was dying and he was ready.

By April I had crossed the Pacheco Pass and found
roosting in the dark branches of the Joshua tree
the fabled magpie— "Had a long tongue and a long tail;
He could both talk and do." This is a holy land,
I thought. At a Sonoco station the attendant,
wiry and dour, said in perfect Okie, "Be careful, son,
a whole family was wiped out right here
just yesterday." At Berenda the fields flooded
for miles in every direction. Arthur's blank sky
stared down at an unruffled inland sea and threatened
to let go. On the way home I cut lilacs
from the divider strip of El Camino Real.
My wife was pregnant. All night we hugged
each other in our narrow bed as the rain
came on in sheets. A family of five, and all
of us were out of work. The dawn was silent.
The black roses, battered, unclenched, the burned petals
floated on the pond beside the playhouse.
Beneath the surface the tiny stunned pike circled
no prey we could see. That was not another life.
I was 29 now and faithless, not the father of the man
I am but the same man who all this day
sat in a still house watching the low clouds massing
in the west, the new winds coming on.
By late afternoon the kids are home from school,
clambering on my front porch, though day
after day I beg them not to. When I go
to the window they race off in mock horror,
daring me to follow. The huge crows that wake

me every morning settle back on the rain spout
next door to caw to the season. I could put them
all in a poem, title it "The Basket of Memory"
as though each image were an Easter egg waiting to hatch,
as though I understood the present and the past
or even why the 8 year old with a cap of blond hair
falling to her shoulders waves to me as she darts
between parked cars and cartwheels into the early dusk.

II

BITTERNESS

Here in February, the fine
dark branches of the almond
begin to sprout tiny clusters
of leaves, sticky to the touch.
Not far off, about the length
of my morning shadow, the grass
is littered with the petals
of the plum that less than
a week ago blazed, a living
candle in the hand of earth.
I was living far off two years
ago, fifteen floors above
119th Street when I heard
a love of my young manhood
had died mysteriously in
a public ward. I did not
go out into the streets to
walk among the cold, sullen
poor of Harlem, I did not
turn toward the filthy window
to question a distant pale sky.
I did not do anything.
The grass is coming back, some
patches already bright, though
at this hour still silvered
with dew. By noon I can stand
sweating in the free air, spading
the difficult clay for the bare
roots of a pear or apple that
will give flower and fruit longer
than I care to think about.

WAKING IN MARCH

Last night, again, I dreamed
my children were back at home,
small boys huddled in their separate beds,
and I went from one to the other
listening to their breathing—regular,
almost soundless—until a white light
hardened against the bedroom wall,
the light of Los Angeles burning south
of here, going at last as we
knew it would. I didn't waken.
Instead the four of us went out
into the front yard and the false dawn
that rose over the Tehachipis and stood
in our bare feet on the wet lawn
as the world shook like a burning house.
Each human voice reached us
without sound, a warm breath on the cheek,
a dry kiss.
                    Why am I so quiet?
This is the end of the world, I am dreaming
the end of the world, and I go from bed
to bed bowing to the small damp heads
of my sons in a bedroom that turns
slowly from darkness to fire. Everyone
else is gone, their last words
reach us in the language of light.
The great eucalyptus trees along the road
swim in the new wind pouring
like water over the mountains. Each day
this is what we waken to, a water
like wind bearing the voices of the world,
the generations of the unborn chanting
in the language of fire. This will be
tomorrow. Why am I so quiet?

FOR THE COUNTRY

THE DREAM

This has nothing to do with war
or the end of the world. She
dreams there are gray starlings
on the winter lawn and the buds
of next year's oranges alongside
this year's oranges, and the sun
is still up, a watery circle
of fire settling into the sky
at dinner time, but there's no
flame racing through the house
or threatening the bed. When she
wakens the phone is ringing
in a distant room, but she
doesn't go to answer it. No
one is home with her, and the cars
passing before the house hiss
in the rain. "My children!" she
almost says, but there are no
longer children at home, there
are no longer those who would
turn to her, their faces running
with tears, and ask her forgiveness.

THE WAR

The Michigan Central Terminal
the day after victory. Her brother
home from Europe after years
of her mother's terror, and he still
so young but now with the dark
shadow of a beard, holding her
tightly among all the others
calling for their wives or girls.

That night in the front room
crowded with family and neighbors—
he was first back on the block—
he sat cross-legged on the floor
still in his wool uniform, smoking
and drinking as he spoke of passing
high over the dark cities she'd
only read about. He'd wanted to
go back again and again. He'd wanted
to do this for the country,
for this—a small house with upstairs
bedrooms—so he'd asked to go
on raid after raid as though
he hungered to kill or be killed.

THE PRESIDENT

Today on television men
will enter space and return,
men she cannot imagine.
Lost in gigantic paper suits,
they move like sea creatures.
A voice will crackle from out
there where no voices are
speaking of the great theater
of conquest, of advancing
beyond the simple miracles
of flight, the small ventures
of birds and beasts. The President
will answer with words she
cannot remember having
spoken ever to anyone.

THE PHONE CALL

She calls Chicago, but no one
is home. The operator asks
for another number but still
no one answers. Together
they try twenty-one numbers,
and at each no one is ever home.
"Can I call Baltimore?" she asks.
She can, but she knows no one
in Baltimore, no one in
St. Louis, Boston, Washington.
She imagines herself standing
before the glass wall high
over Lake Shore Drive, the cars
below fanning into the city.
East she can see all the way
to Gary and the great gray clouds
of exhaustion rolling over
the lake where her vision ends.
This is where her brother lives.
At such height there's nothing,
no birds, no growing, no noise.
She leans her sweating forehead
against the cold glass, shudders,
and puts down the receiver.

THE GARDEN

Wherever she turns her garden
is alive and growing. The thin
spears of wild asparagus, shaft
of tulip and flag, green stain
of berry buds along the vines,
even in the eaten leaf of

27

pepper plants and clipped stalk
of snap bean. Mid-afternoon
and already the grass is dry
under the low sun. Bluejay
and dark capped juncos hidden
in dense foliage waiting
the sun's early fall, when she
returns alone to hear them
call and call back, and finally
in the long shadows settle
down to rest and to silence
in the sudden rising chill.

THE GAME

Two boys are playing ball
in the backyard, throwing it
back and forth in the afternoon's
bright sunshine as a black mongrel
big as a shepherd races
from one to the other. She
hides behind the heavy drapes
in her dining room and listens,
but they're too far. Who are
they? They move about her yard
as though it were theirs. Are they
the sons of her sons? They've
taken off their shirts, and she
sees they're not boys at all—
a dark smudge of hair rises
along the belly of one—, and now
they have the dog down thrashing
on his back, snarling and flashing
his teeth, and they're laughing.

AFTER DINNER

She's eaten dinner talking
back to the television, she's
had coffee and brandy, done
the dishes and drifted into
and out of sleep over a book
she found beside the couch. It's
time for bed, but she goes
instead to the front door, unlocks
it, and steps onto the porch.
Behind her she can hear only
the silence of the house. The lights
throw her shadow down the stairs
and onto the lawn, and she walks
carefully to meet it. Now she's
standing in the huge, whispering
arena of night, hearing her
own breath tearing out of her
like the cries of an animal.
She could keep going into
whatever the darkness brings,
she could find a presence there
her shaking hands could hold
instead of each other.

SLEEP

A dark sister lies beside her
all night, whispering
that it's not a dream, that fire
has entered the spaces between
one face and another.
There will be no wakening.
When she wakens, she can't

catch her own breath, so she yells
for help. It comes in the form
of sleep. They whisper
back and forth, using new words
that have no meaning
to anyone. The aspen shreds
itself against her window.
The oranges she saw that day
in her yard explode
in circles of oil, the few stars
quiet and darken. They go on,
two little girls up long past
their hour, playing in bed.

THESE STREETS

If I told you that the old woman
named Ida Bellow was shot to death
for no more than $5 and that a baby
of eighteen months saw it all from
where she wakened on the same bed
but can't tell because she can't speak,
you'd say I was making it up. If I
took you by the hand and led you down
street after street until we arrived
at a door that seemed no different
from the rest and entered to behold
the flowered coverlet not yet washed
on the single iron bed, the calendar
stopped on the second Sunday in February,
the cluttered three-burner stove, the sink
of cracked dishes, the old wheelchair
Ida used to get around, you'd stand
in the middle of the bare floor as far
from everything as you could get
listening to the cracked window moan
and see nothing. The baby's mother—
she's only nineteen—says she'll raise
the baby by herself now Ida's gone,
and she's not going to cry about it,
no, not in front of us two. No.
It was Cabin, the neighbor lady says,
Ida raised him from a child, raised
him up to this, and raised his sisters,
too, and she counts them off on her fingers,
one, two, three, four, she counts them off.

*

Why did we come here to begin with?
There was a pond once, and a path
small creatures took into the woods.
Brown warblers called down the first light,

and we woke with it to the long days
bursting with sudden anemones, iris
growing wild, purple throated finches
as small as canaries tumbling the air.
In late summer tall grasses grew, and we
hid side by side from the heavy sun, hid
in our own neat bed of broken reeds,
a little cup the earth made for us.
Our breath came and went. The sky passed
overhead still unstreaked by the geese
heading down from Canada, unmarred
by anything except the clouds massing
toward late afternoon. Yes, it was August
once, and the west wind was warm, even
at sunset. When I closed my eyes I
slept, when I opened them I saw a river
of stars overflowing their black bowl.

*

Six floor walk-ups, half the windows
boarded up, the doorways bricked over.
Still some families hanging on, kids
flood into the ruined streets morning
after morning on their way to school.
When it dies down, stray animals pick
over the rubbish, a family of four cats
exits the innards of a blooming sofa.
Between 9:30 and afternoon not
a single car starts up or passes down
the street. In the corner grocery
three lopsided apples on special,
30 cents each. The woman says it's
a good neighborhood, ain't no violence
here, ain't no trouble. A man comes
out of the back room and stares
at me until I look away. No one

speaks, not even the radio. The light
of the world filters down from shelves
of Brillo, bright packages of detergent,
paper diapers, roach motels, white
stale saltless crackers. Moment
by yellow moment the day ticks into
the past, and no one tries anything.

III

AT BESSEMER

19 years old and going nowhere,
I got a ride to Bessemer and walked
the night road toward Birmingham
passing dark groups of men cursing
the end of a week like every week.
Out of town I found a small grove
of trees, high narrow pines, and I
sat back against the trunk of one
as the first rains began slowly.
South, the lights of Bessemer glowed
as though a new sun rose there,
but it was midnight and another shift
tooled the rolling mills. I must
have slept awhile, for someone
else was there beside me. I could
see a cigarette's soft light,
and once a hand grazed mine, man
or woman's I never knew. Slowly
I could feel the darkness fill
my eyes and the dream that came was
of a bright world where sunlight
fell on the long even rows of houses
and I looked down from great height
at a burned world I believed
I never had to enter. When
the true sun rose I was stiff
and wet, and there beside me was
the small white proof that someone
rolled and smoked and left me there
unharmed, truly untouched.
A hundred yards off I could hear
cars on the highway. A life
was calling to be lived, but how
and why I had still to learn.

DOG POEM

Fierce and stupid all dogs are
and some worse. I learned this
early by walking to school
unarmed and unprepared
for big city life, which they
had been bred to for centuries.
The chow who barred my way
snarling through his black lips
taught me I was tiny and helpless
and that if he grew more determined
I could neither talk nor fight,
and my school books, my starred exams,
my hand-woven woolen mittens, a gift
of my grandmother, would fall
to the puddled sidewalk and
at best my cold sack of lunch
might buy me a few moments
to prepare my soul before I slept.
I inched by him, smelling the breath
hot and sour as old clothes.
He did nothing but rave, rising
toward me on his hind legs
and choking against the collar
which miraculously held. Later,
years later, delivering mail
on bicycle in the new California,
I was set on by a four-footed moron
who tore at my trousers even
as I drummed small rocks off
his head. I dreamed that head
became soup, and the small eyes stared
out into the bright dining room
of the world's great dog lovers,
and they ate and wept by turns
while I pedaled through the quiet streets
bringing bad news and good to
the dogless citizenry of Palo Alto.

The shepherd dog without sheep
who guards the gates to sleep wakens
each night as my tiny boat
begins to drift out on the waters
of silence. He bays and bays
until the lights come on, and I
sit up sweating and alarmed, alone
in the bed I came to call home.
Now I am weary of fighting and carry
at all times small hard wafers
of dried essence of cat to purchase
a safe way among the fanged masters
of the avenues. If I must come back
to this world let me do so as the lion
of legend, but striped like an alley cat.
Let me saunter back the exact way
I came turning each corner to face
the barking hosts of earth until they
scurry for cover or try pathetically
to climb the very trees that earlier
they peed upon and shamed. Let their pads
slide upon the glassy trunks,
weight them down with exercise books,
sacks of post cards, junk mail, ads,
dirty magazines, give them three kids
in the public schools, hemorrhoids,
a tiny fading hope to rise above
the power of unleashed, famished animals
and postmasters, give them two big feet
and shoes that don't fit, and dull work
five days a week. Give them my life.

A THEORY OF PROSODY

When Nellie, my old pussy
cat, was still in her prime,
she would sit behind me
as I wrote, and when the line
got too long she'd reach
one sudden black foreleg down
and paw at the moving hand,
the offensive one. The first
time she drew blood I learned
it was poetic to end
a line anywhere to keep her
quiet. After all, many mornings she'd gotten to the chair
long before I was even up.
Those nights I couldn't sleep
she'd come and sit in my lap
to calm me. So I figured
I owed her the short cat line.
She's dead now almost nine years,
and before that there was one
during which she faked attention
and I faked obedience.
Isn't that what it's about—
pretending there's an alert cat
who leaves nothing to chance.

IN A LIGHT TIME

The alder shudders
in the April winds
off the moon. No one
is awake and yet
sunlight streams across
the hundred still beds
of the public wards
for children. At ten
do we truly sleep
in a blessed sleep
guarded by angels
and social workers?
Do we dream of gold
found in secret trunks
in familiar rooms?
Do we talk to cats
and dogs? I think not.
I think when I was
ten I was almost
an adult, slightly
less sentimental
than now and better
with figures. No one
could force me to cry,
nothing could convince
me of God's concern
for America
much less the fall of
a sparrow. I spit
into the wind, even
on mornings like this,
the air clear, the sky
utterly silent,
the fresh light flooding
across bed after
bed as though something
were reaching blindly—

for we are blindest
in sunlight—for hands
to take and eyelids
to caress and bless
before they open
to the alder gone
still and the winds hushed,
before the children
waken separately
into their childhoods.

I SING THE BODY ELECTRIC

People sit numbly at the counter
waiting for breakfast or service.
Today it's Hartford, Connecticut
more than twenty-five years after
the last death of Wallace Stevens.
I have come in out of the cold
and wind of a Sunday morning
of early March, and I seem to be
crying, but I'm only freezing
and unpeeled. The waitress brings
me hot tea in a cracked cup,
and soon it's all over my paper,
and so she refills it. I read
slowly in *The New York Times*
that poems are dying in Iowa,
Missoula, on the outskirts of Reno,
in the shopping galleries of Houston.
We should all go to the grave
of the unknown poet while the rain
streaks our notebooks or stand
for hours in the freezing winds
off the lost books of our fathers
or at least until we can no longer
hold our pencils. Men keep coming
in and going out, and two of them
recall the great dirty fights
between Willy Pep and Sandy Sadler,
between little white perfection
and death in red plaid trunks.
I want to tell them I saw
the last fight, I rode out
to Yankee Stadium with two deserters
from the French Army of Indochina
and back with a drunken priest
and both ways the whole train
smelled of piss and vomit, but no
one would believe me. Those are

the true legends better left to die.
In my black rain coat I go back
out into the gray morning and dare
the cars on North Indemnity Boulevard
to hit me, but no one wants trouble
at this hour. I have crossed
a continent to bring these citizens
the poems of the snowy mountains,
of the forges of hopelessness,
of the survivors of wars they
never heard of and won't believe.
Nothing is alive in this tunnel
of winds of the end of winter
except the last raging of winter,
the cats peering smugly from the homes
of strangers, and the great stunned sky
slowly settling like a dark cloud
lined only with smaller dark clouds.

PICTURE POSTCARD FROM
THE OTHER WORLD

Since I don't know who will be reading
this or even if it will be read, I must
invent someone on the other end
of eternity, a distant cousin laboring
under the same faint stars I labored
all those unnumbered years ago. I make you
like me in everything I can— a man
or woman in middle years who having
lost whatever faiths he held goes on
with only the faith that even more
will be lost. Like me a wanderer,
someone with a taste for coastal towns
sparkling in the cold winter sun, boardwalks
without walkers, perfect beaches shrouded
in the dense fogs of December, morning cafes
before the second customer arrives,
the cats have been fed, and the proprietor
stops muttering into the cold dishwater.
I give you the gift of language, my gift
and no more, so that wherever you go
words fall around you meaning no more
than the full force of their making, and you
translate the clicking of teeth against
teeth and tongue as morning light spilling
into the enclosed squares of a white town,
breath drawn in and held as the ocean
when no one sees it, the waves still,
the fishing boats drift in a calm beyond sleep.
The gift of sleep, too, and the waking
from it day after day without knowing
why the small sunlit room with its single bed,
white counterpane going yellow, and bare floor
holds itself with such assurance
while the flaming nebulae of dust
swirl around you. And the sense not to ask.
Like me you rise immediately and sit

on the bed's edge and let whatever dream
of a childhood home or a rightful place
you had withdraw into the long shadows
of the tilted wardrobe and the one chair.
Before you've even washed your face you
see it on the bedoilied chiffonier— there,
balanced precariously on the orange you bought
at yesterday's market and saved for now.
Someone entered soundlessly while you slept
and left you sleeping and left this postcard
from me and thought to close the door
with no more fuss than the moon makes.
There's your name in black ink in a hand
as familiar as your own and not
your own, and the address even you
didn't know you'd have an hour before
you got it. When you turn it over,
there it is, not the photo of a star,
or the bright sailboats your sister would
have chosen or the green urban meadows
my brother painted. What is it? It could be
another planet just after its birth
except that at the center the colors
are earth colors. It could be the cloud
that formed above the rivers of our blood,
the one that brought rain to a dry time
or took wine from a hungry one. It could
be my way of telling you that I too
burned and froze by turns and the face I
came to was more dirt than flame, it
could be the face I put on everything,
or it could be my way of saying
nothing and saying it perfectly.

IV

A WALK WITH TOM JEFFERSON

Between the freeway
      and the gray conning towers
of the ballpark, miles
      of mostly vacant lots, once
a neighborhood of small
      two-storey wooden houses—
dwellings for immigrants
      from Ireland, Germany,
Poland, West Virginia,
      Mexico, Dodge Main.
A little world with only
      three seasons, or so we said—
one to get tired, one to get
      old, one to die.
No one puts in irises,
      and yet before March passes
the hard green blades push
      their way through
where firm lawns once were.
      The trunks of beech and locust
darken, the light new branches
      take the air. You can
smell the sticky sap rising
      in the maples, smell it
even over the wet stink
      of burned houses.
On this block seven houses
      are still here to be counted,
and if you count the shacks
      housing illegal chickens,
the pens for dogs, the tiny
      pig sty that is half cave . . .
and if you count them you can
      count the crows' nest
in the high beech tree
      at the corner, and you can
regard the beech tree itself

                    bronzing in mid-morning light
as the mast of the great ship
              sailing us all back
into the 16th century
              or into the present age's
final discovery. (Better
              perhaps not to speak
of final anything, for
              this place was *finally* retired,
the books thrown away
              when after the town exploded
in '67 these houses
              were plundered for whatever
they had. Some burned
              to the ground, some
hung open, doorless, wide-eyed
              until hauled off
by the otherwise unemployable
              citizens of the county
to make room for the triumphant
              return of Mad Anthony Wayne,
Père Marquette, Cadillac,
              the badger, the wolverine,
the meadow lark, the benign
              long toothed bi-ped
with nothing on his mind.)
              During baseball season
the neighborhood's a thriving
              business for anyone
who can make change
              and a cardboard sign
that reads "Parking $3."
              He can stand on the curb
directing traffic and pretending
              the land is his.
On August nights I come
              out here after ten

and watch the light rise
        from the great gray bowl
of the stadium, watch it catch
        a scrap of candy wrapper
in the wind, a soiled napkin
        or a peanut shell and turn
it into fire or the sound
        of fire as the whole world
holds its breath. In the last
        inning 50,000
pulling at the night
        air for one last scream.
They can drain the stars
        of light. No one
owns any of this.
        It's condemned,
but the money for the execution
        ran out years ago.
Money is a dream, part
        of the lost past.
Joe Louis grew up a few miles
        east of here and attended
Bishop Elementary.
        No one recalls
a slender, dumbfounded
        boy afraid of his fifth grade
home room teacher. Tom Jefferson
        —"Same name as the other one"—
remembers Joe at seventeen
        all one sweltering summer
unloading bales of rags
        effortlessly from the trucks
that parked in the alley
        behind Wolfe Sanitary Wiping Cloth.
"Joe was beautiful,"
        is all he says, and we two
go dumb replaying Joe's

51

glide across the ring
as he corners Schmeling
and prepares to win
World War II. Like Joe
Tom was up from Alabama,
like Joe he didn't talk
much then, and even now
he passes a hand across
his mouth when speaking
of the $5 day that lured
his father from the cotton fields
and a one-room shack the old folks
talked about until
they went home first
to visit and later to die.
Early afternoon behind
his place, Tom's gathering up
the remnants of this year's
garden—the burned
tomato plants and the hardy
runners of summer squash
that dug into the chalky
soil and won't let go.
He stuffs the dried remains
into a supermarket shopping cart
to haul off to an empty block.
The zinnias are left,
the asters in browns and dirty
yellows, tough petalled
autumn blooms, even a few
sticky green rose buds
climbing a telephone pole.
Alabama is not so far back
it's lost in a swirl
of memory. "I can see trees
behind the house. I do
believe I still feel

winter mornings, all of us
        getting up from one bed
but for what I don't know."
        He tips his baseball cap
to the white ladies passing
        back the way we've come.
"We all come for $5
        a day and we got this!"
His arms spread wide to
        include block after block
of dumping grounds,
        old couches and settees
burst open, the white innards
        gone gray, cracked
and mangled chifforobes
        that long ago gave up
their secrets, yellow wooden
        ice boxes yawning
at the sky, their breath
        still fouled with years
of eating garlic sausage
        and refried beans,
the shattered rib cages
        of beds that couldn't hold
our ordinary serviceable dreams,
        blue mattresses stained
in earnest, the cracked
        toilet seats of genius,
whole market counters
        that once contained the red meats
we couldn't get enough of,
        burned out electric motors,
air conditioners
        we suffocated, and over all
an arctic wind from Canada
        which carries off
the final faint unseeable

                    spasm of the desire
         to be human and brings down
                    the maple and elm leaves
         of early October. If you follow
                    their trail of burnished arrows
         scuttling across curbs and cracked
                    sidewalks they'll lead
         you to the cellar hole
                    of something or someone
         called Dogman. "Making do,"
                    says Tom Jefferson.
         His neighbors swear
                    someone runs on all fours
         with his dog packs. They claim
                    they can tell when
         their own dogs feel the pull
                    of the wild ones.
         The women talk of lost
                    house cats grown to the size
         of cougars. They've heard them
                    crashing through the dense
         underbrush of the dumping
                    ground and found
         huge paw tracks in the snow,
                    the remains of drunks
         and children caught out
                    after dark, nothing but clean bones
         revealed under ice when
                    the spring rains come back.
         "There ain't no kids
                    around here," says Tom,
         "But if there were, the bones
                    be about the same size."
         Tom has seen vapor rising
                    through the missing floorboards,
         clouds of it, and maybe
                    animals and man

together producing a new
> variety of steam heat.
Even I have seen a brutish
> black mongrel Dane
in late afternoon, his coat
> snow flecked, rising
on his hind legs to over
> seven feet, hanging
over fences, peering in windows
> as though he yearned
to come back to what
> we were. Winter's in everything
we say— it's coming on—we see
> it in the mad swirl
of leaves and newspapers
> doing their dances.
We feel it as iron
> in the wind. We could escape,
each of us feels in
> his shuddering heart, take
the bridge south to Canada,
> but we don't. Instead we
hunker down, slump a little
> lower in our trousers,
and go slow. One night soon
> I'll waken to a late quiet
and go out to see all this
> transformed, each junked car,
each dumping ground and battered
> hovel a hill
of mounded snow, every scrap
> of ugliness redeemed
under the light of a street lamp
> or the moon. From the dark tower
of the Renaissance Center Ford built
> to look down
on our degradation to the great

Ford plant downriver blowing
its black breath in the face
of creation, the one at Rouge
where he broke first our backs
and then the rest, everything
silent, suspended in a new world
like no other. For a moment
a few stars come out to share
this witness. I won't believe it,
but Tom will. Tom Jefferson
is a believer.
You can't plant winter vegetables
if you aren't,
you can't plant anything, except
maybe radishes.
You don't have to believe
anything to grow
radishes. Early August he's got
sweet corn
two feet above his head,
he stretches
his arm to show where
they grow to.
Tomatoes "remind you what tomatoes
taste like."
He was planting before the Victory Gardens.
His mother brought
the habit up from Alabama. She was
growing greens
behind the house no matter how small
her strip of land,
cosmos beside the back door,
early things
like pansies along the fence.
"Why she could go
into a bare field and find
the purple flags,

wild, bring them home, half-
     dead dirty chicks
on the palm of her hand, and they'd
     grow. I could
never do that, I gave up trying
     fifty years ago."
It didn't take FDR
     and "the war effort"
to make a believer out of Tom.
     When he went off to war
his son Tom Jr. took over
     the garden and did
a job, the same son went off
     to Korea and didn't
come home, the son he seldom talks
     about, just as he
seldom talks about his three years
     in the Seabees
building airstrips so we could
     bomb Japan, doing
the war work he did at home
     for less pay.
A father puts down a spade, his son
     picks it up,
"That's Biblical," he says,
     "the son goes off,
the father takes up the spade
     again, that's Biblical."
He'd leave for work in the cold
     dark of December.
Later, out the high broken windows
     at Dodge Main
he'd see the snow falling
     silently and know
it was falling on the dark petals
     of the last rose,
know his wife was out

                    back hunched
in her heavy gray sweater
            letting those first flakes
slowly settle into
                water on the warm
red flesh of the dime store
            plants Tom Jr.
put in on his own.
                Later he'd come home
in the early dark
            with snow on his hair,
tracking the dirty
            snow on her rug—
they say the dogs yellow
            it before it hits
the ground—and she would
            say nothing.
"That's Biblical," he says.
            "We couldn't even look
near each other
            for fear of how
one might make the other cry.
            That's Biblical,
knowing the other so well
            you know yourself,
being careful the way she was
            never to say nothing
or show the least sign."
            Tom picks a maple leaf
stiff backed and brown
            from the gutter,
holds it against the distant
            pale sky streaked
with contrails. Maybe even
            war is Biblical, maybe
even the poor white
            fighting the poor black

in this city for the same
           gray concrete housing,
the same gray jobs
           they both came
north for, maybe that's
           Biblical, the way
the Canaanites and the Philistines
           fought the Israelites,
and the Israelites killed
           the Amalakites
always for the same land.
           "God wanted Saul
to kill them down to the last lamb.
           He didn't,
and he went crazy. Back
           in the riots of '42
they did not kill us down
           to the last lamb.
They needed us making airfields
           the way they needed us
making Fords before the war,
           maybe that's why
they went crazy." There at the end
           of the street is his house,
his since he came home
           and could never leave.
The wisteria along the side
           has grown to the thickness
of his own wrist, the back yard
           is roses still, squash
coming on, onions in late
           bloom to be tricked
by the first cold, potatoes
           hidden underground,
they think, forever.
           "It's Biblical.
The way David plays for Saul so he

can weep, and later
when his turn comes David
            weeps for Absalom.
It's Biblical, you cry,
            it's Biblical you don't,
either way. That's Biblical."
            What commandment
was broken to bring God's
            wrath down on these streets,
what did we wrong, going
            about our daily lives,
to work at all hours until
            the work dried up,
then sitting home until home
            became a curse
with the yellow light
            of afternoon falling
with all the weight of final
            judgement, I can't say.
It's Biblical, this season
            of color coming
to its end, the air swirling
            in tiny cyclones
of brown and red, the air
            swelling my lungs,
banging about my ears so that
            I almost think I hear
Tom say "Absalom" again, a name
            owed to autumn
and the autumn of his hopes.
            It's Biblical,
the little pyres pluming
            the afternoon gray and blue
on these corners, the calm
            of these childless streets,
a dog howling from a distant
            block, another answering,

the calls of the chained animals
            going back and forth
so plaintive and usual no one
            hears. The sparrows
fan out across the grassless yards
            busily seeking
whatever seeds the cold winds
            burst forth, and this
day is coming to its end
            with only the smallest
winter birds to keep
            the vigil. "We need
this season," Tom has said,
            but Tom believes
the roots need cold,
            the earth needs to turn
to ice and snow so a new fire
            can start up in the heart
of all that grows.
            He doesn't say that.
He doesn't say the heart
            of ice is fire waiting,
he doesn't say the new seed
            nestles in the old,
waiting, frozen, for the land
            to thaw, and even these streets
of cracking blacktop long gone gray,
            the seven junked cars
the eye can note collapsed
            on slashed tires, their insides
drawn out for anything, he doesn't
            say all this is a lost land,
it's Biblical. He parks his chromed
            shopping cart under the porch,
brushes the dirt and leaves
            from his worn corduroy—
six feet of man, unbowed—

and locks the knee-high gate
of his fence that could
        hold back no one,
smiles and says the one word,
        "Tomorrow," and goes in.
Later he'll put the porch light on,
        though no one's coming.
The crazy Indian colors
        are blooming as the sun
begins to go, deep maroons
        they tell us are the signs
of all the earth we've pumped
        into the sky.
The same rich browns the ground
        reveals after rain,
the veins of orange I've uncovered
        digging the yard
spring after spring. Never once
        have I found the least sign
that this was once the Indian's
        ground, perhaps a holy land,
not a single arrow head
        or shard, though I
have caught a sudden glint of
        what I didn't know
while turning over dirt I swore
        was never turned before
only to kneel to a bottle cap
        polished down
to anonymity or a wad
        of tinfoil
from an empty pack
        of Luckys, curled
to the shape of whatever
        vanished human hand
tossed it off. We were not
        idle hands. Still a kid

when I worked nights
       on the milling machines
at Cadillac transmission,
       another kid just up
from West Virginia asked me
       what was we making,
and I answered, I'm making
       2.25 an hour,
don't know what you're
       making, and he had
to correct me, gently, what was
       we making out of
this here metal, and I didn't know.
       Whatever it was we
made, we made of earth. Amazing earth,
       amazed perhaps
by all it's given us,
       as amazed as I
who stood one afternoon
       forty years ago
at a railroad crossing
       near Joy Road
as the Sherman tanks passed
       two to a flat-bed car,
on their way to a war,
       their long guns
frowning down identically, they
       passed some twenty minutes
or more while the tracks groaned,
       the trestle snapped
and sighed with so much stubborn
       weight of our going.
Later, in the forge room
       at Chevy, now a man,
still making what I never knew,
       I stood in the silence
of the great presses slamming

home, the roar of earth
striking the fired earth, the reds
          searing their glowing image
into the eye and brain,
          the oranges and roses
blooming in the mind long
          after, even in sleep.
What were we making out
          of this poor earth good
for so much giving and taking?
          (Beets the size of fists
by the thousands, cabbages
          as big as brains
year after year, whole cribs
          of peppers, great lakes
of sweet corn tumbling
          by the trailer load,
it gave and gave, and whatever
          we had it took.)
The place was called Chevy
          Gear & Axle—
it's gone now, gone to earth
          like so much here—
so perhaps we actually made
          gears and axles
for the millions of Chevies
          long dead or still to die.
It said that, "Chevrolet
          Gear & Axle"
right on the checks they paid
          us with, so I can
half-believe that's what we
          were making way back then.

Philip Levine was born in 1928 in Detroit and was formally educated there, at the public schools and at Wayne University. After a succession of stupid jobs he left the city for good, living in various parts of the country before he settled in Fresno, California, where he now teaches. *The Names of the Lost* won the Lenore Marshall Award for the best book of poetry published by an American in 1976. Three of his books have been nominated for the National Book Critics Circle Award, and two of them, *Ashes* and *7 Years from Somewhere*, have received it. *Ashes* also received the American Book Award in 1980. His *Selected Poems* appeared in 1984. In 1987 he received the Ruth Lilly Poetry Prize "for distinguished poetic achievements," awarded by *Poetry* magazine and The American Council for the Arts.

A NOTE ON THE TYPE

This book was set in Monticello, a Linotype re-
vival of the original Roman No. 1 cut by Archi-
bald Binny and cast in 1796 by the Philadelphia type foundry Binny & Ronaldson. The face
was named Monticello in honor of its use in the
monumental fifty-volume *Papers of Thomas Jefferson*, published by Princeton University Press.
Monticello is a transitional type design, embody-
ing certain features of Bulmer and Baskerville,
but it is a distinguished face in its own right.

Composition by Heritage Printers, Inc., Charlotte, N. C.
Printed and bound by Halliday Lithographers,
West Hanover, Massachusetts
Designed by Harry Ford